Russell's Journal

Trust

Russell's Journal

Trust

by

Mary A. Payne

Illustrated by Phyllis Parker Whiteside

DORRANCE PUBLISHING CO., INC.
PITTSBURGH, PENNSYLVANIA 15222

Dedicated to my mother,
Rosina Virgie Payne,
who taught God's moral values
to her children and grandchildren.

Table of Contents

Acknowledgments

Rose T. Montgomery, my sister and an elementary school teacher, for her ideas and inspiration.

Johnnie L. Montgomery II, my nephew, a college freshman who named Russell and provided views from a male perspective.

LaMont Daniels, who graciously offered valuable insight and suggestions.

Marjorie Thomas for her prayers and encouragement. She was the first person to read this book and request copies.

Most of all I would like to thank God, whose influence through the Holy Spirit inspired this work.

Introduction

Children in our society have a need to become familiar with moral truths based on biblical principles. "They should be brought up with the loving discipline the Lord approves of along with godly suggestions and godly advice."[1]

Parents should provide love, food, clothing, shelter, support, safety and stability, in an environment which encourages open expression of thoughts and feelings. "Children should obey their parents for it is the right thing to do and because God has placed parents in authority over their children."[2]

Society's moral values change but the moral values of God will never change. They remain constant forever and ever.

In this story, Russell listened to his parents and minister and learned how to deal with a difficult situation.

Hi, my name is Russell. I am seven years old. I go to King Elementary, in the second grade. I live with my mama and daddy, and two brothers and sisters. Ronnie is sixteen years old, Steve is ten. Geri is fourteen and Stacie is five.

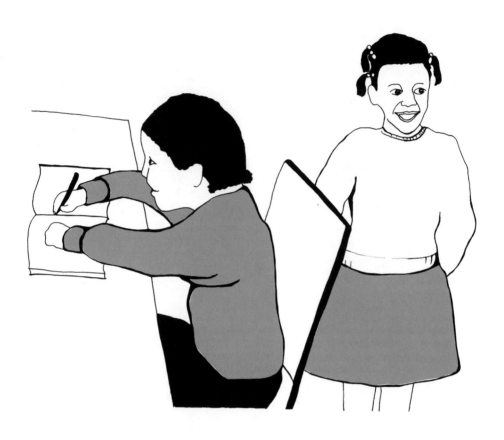

I'm just writing in my journal. My daddy gave it to me last week. My sister Geri laughs and says it's a diary, but it's not. Everyday I write down what happened to me and how I feel. I hide it under my mattress so Geri can't read it. I write it just for me. Sometimes I talk about what's in it. Why did Daddy give the journal to me? Well, it's a long story, but I'll tell You if You can keep a secret, okay?

Last Monday in school, Susie sat next to me at story-time. She's okay, I guess. Well, I kinda like her, okay? I smiled every time she looked at me and I felt really stupid. She didn't say anything and I didn't either. I'm really glad the teacher didn't ask me anything about the story she read, 'cause I didn't hear it. Don't laugh, okay? All I knew was that I liked sitting next to Susie.

At lunchtime my friend Ernie sat with me and asked me what was wrong with me. I told him nothing and hoped he would not ask again. As I drank my milk, my eyes searched the cafeteria for her. When I found her, I choked on my milk. Ernie was watching me with a puzzled look on his face. He finally asked, "Why are you staring at her?" I responded, "At who, what are you talking about?" "Susie," he responded.

I told him to be quiet and promised to tell him later. He agreed.

At recess I told Ernie everything. He laughed and teased me a little. That wasn't so bad. It kinda felt good to tell somebody. But when I saw him whispering to Susie I could have died. She looked at me and smiled. I couldn't believe Ernie would tell her what I said. Susie whispered to the other girls and they all looked at me and laughed. I was mad at Ernie and Susie for laughing at me.

After school, Ernie came to me and said, "I told her for you, Russell," and smiled, proud of what he'd done. I was really mad at Ernie now, 'cause he thought he was helping me. I merely said, "Shut up Ernie," and walked away from him. I heard him repeat, "What's wrong, Russell?" but I kept walking.

Well, by the time I got home, I was crying. Don't tell nobody that, especially Ernie, Okay? Daddy held me on his lap and I told him the whole story.

When I stopped crying, Daddy talked to me about trust. He asked me to name people that I could trust. As I started naming people, Mama came in and sat with us.

I want to share with you what my daddy and mama said.

Who Should You Trust

Sometimes it is not always easy to know what to do. Talk to your mom and dad or an adult that you trust about anything that you don't understand. For everyone, there are two main rules:

1. Never trust a stranger
2. Always trust in God

Do Not Trust Strangers!

A stranger can be a man or a woman. Do not talk to a stranger or get near them. Do not take anything they offer you. Run away, tell an adult that you trust, and tell your parents.

I can trust some strangers.

Police

Mama and Daddy say policemen are our friends. Their job is to keep everybody safe. Sometimes my friends talk badly about policemen and call them names. Whenever we have a car accident, we call the police. When there is a robbery, burglary, or you're scared at home, the police are called.

A policeman is a stranger.

I can trust the policeman.

Ambulances

I was with Mama and Daddy on our way home from the store one night. On the street ahead, we could see wrecked cars, tow trucks, two ambulances, and three police cars. The paramedics were busy working on people lying on the ground. Mama and Daddy say people's lives are saved because of emergency care they get at accident scenes.

Ambulance drivers are strangers.

I can trust paramedics.

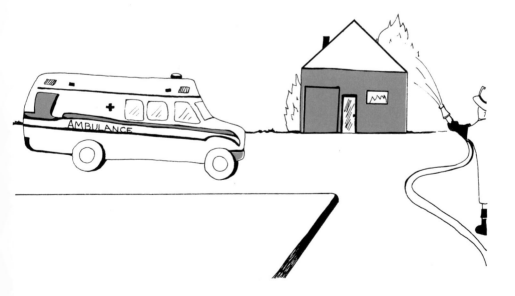

Fire Department

One day I saw two fire trucks at my neighbor's house when I got home from school. Big water hoses were spread up and down the street. A garage had caught on fire and the firemen were busy spraying water on it. The hoses looked really heavy. Sometimes two firemen were holding one hose. Daddy says firemen sometimes rescue people from burning houses.

Firemen are strangers.

I can trust firemen.

Family

We do a lot together. Sometimes Grandma and Grandpa are with us. Dad really likes cookouts. He's getting better at barbecuing, too. Mama and Daddy sit down and talk to all of us kids together, once a week. We share how we feel about everything. I like those times. When we have problems, they're there. My brothers and sisters help me sometimes.

I trust **my family.**

Friend

My best friend is Ernie. We live on the same street. We have lots of fun together. Sometimes we play at my house, sometimes at his house. I like Ernie because he is nice to me. He lets me play with his things. He helps me when I need help and sometimes when I don't. I just like to be around him. We talk all the time. He didn't mean to tell my secret. I am his best friend too. We play with my toys. I help Ernie when he needs me and I have never told his secrets.

Ernie can trust me.

Neighbors

Mrs. Smith lives down the street. She's really old, about eighty-five, and has this really neat cane. Well, sometimes when I see her get out of the cab, I run and carry her groceries into her house for her. It makes her happy and, well she's real nice to my mama and daddy. She gives me cookies, really good ones.

I can trust Mrs. Smith.

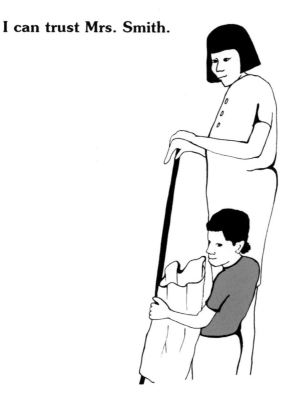

Minister

My minister, Reverend Brown, always has time for kids. He says, "The children of today are the church of tomorrow." He preached on Sunday about trusting the Lord. He said it is better to trust in the Lord than to trust in man.

I can trust my minister.

School Crossing Guard

Mr. Jones is retired from his job at the post office. Now he works everyday as the crossing guard at my school. The kids like him. He's nice. When I have a problem with a friend or something, he helps me. He never tells anyone my problems. He reminds me of my grandpa with that funny little laugh.

I trust Mr. Jones.

Teacher

My teacher, Miss Bell, is okay even though she made the whole class clean out their desks 'cause one kid had a worm in his. I wish I had a worm, too.

Miss Bell brings me books about astronauts and lets me read when I finish my work early. She tells us kids that we can be anything we really want to be. That makes me feel good.

I can trust Miss Bell.

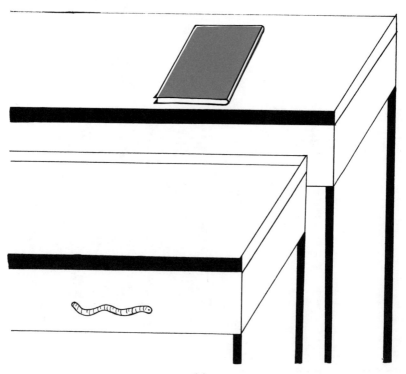

Doctors and Nurses

When I was sick a long time ago, Mama took me to the doctor's office. Dr. Brewer and his nurse, Miss Carter, were very nice. After they checked me, I got a shot. It burned a little but it didn't hurt that bad. I felt a lot better the next day.

I trust my doctor and nurse.

God

Daddy and Mama say it's nice to have all these people who can help you and who are nice to you. Even though people care about you and will do nice things for you, there are times when they cannot be there or they don't know what you need.

God is always with you, He loves you very much, and He knows everything. God loves us so much that He sent his only son from Heaven to save all men. God's son's name is **Jesus Christ**.

I trust God and His son, Jesus.

I tell my friend Ernie about Jesus. Ernie asks a lot of questions. Some answers I learned in Sunday school, church, or from mama and Daddy. Sometimes I have to ask Reverend Brown.

Here's how I answered Ernie's questions:

Ernie: How do you know Jesus is God's son?

Russell: When John the Baptist baptized Jesus in the Jordan
           River, God's spirit landed on Jesus and a voice
           from Heaven said, "This is my beloved son in
           whom I'm well pleased."³

Ernie: Wow! Is that in the Bible?

Russell: Yeah.

Ernie: How do you know that Jesus hears you when you
           tell Him your secrets?

Russell: Ernie, God knows everything, even the hardest math
           problem in college.

Ernie: Wow!

Russell: Reverend Brown says "all you have to do is ask God
           for anything and God will give it to you,"⁴ if it's
           okay for you to have it.

Ernie: What do you mean, if it's okay?

Russell: Reverend Brown says God is our father and just like
           a daddy, He won't give you anything that you
           shouldn't have.

Ernie: Like what?

Russell: Remember when I asked Daddy for that motorcycle?

Ernie: Yeah.

Russell: Daddy said no 'cause I was too young. He won't let
          me drive either. Ronnie gets to drive to school.

Ernie: Oh, Yeah.

Russell: Anyway, if God will give you what you ask for, He
          has to hear you ask. Right?

Ernie: Sounds right to me.

Russell: When you talk to God, That's called prayer.

Ernie: I say my prayers every night.

Russell: Me too.

Daddy told me that the next time I tell Ernie a secret to ask
him not to tell. I did forget to tell him it was a secret. I'm not
angry with him any more. I told him I was sorry for getting mad
and not telling him it was a secret. Ernie told me he was sorry
he told Susie. He didn't know it was a secret. We agreed to
keep each other's secrets. We are still best friends, and we trust
each other. I still like Susie. She doesn't laugh at me any more.
Her friends don't either.

Now you know why Daddy gave me this journal. I can put
my secret thoughts in it when I don't feel like sharing.

It's fun to have secrets that you can share with others and
it's fun to have secrets just between you and **God**.

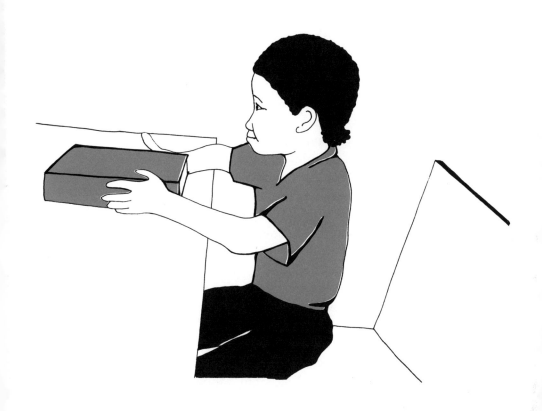

Trust Him

I'll tell you **why I** trust the Lord
    And you must listen close
I trust Him for He stays with me
    He really is the most.
He loves his people everywhere
    North, East, South, and West
God has no favorite ones, you see
    He loves us all the best
He never leaves you all alone
    He's always by your side
And When I know He's near to me
    I feel so satisfied.
When life is hard and friends are rare
    And people say that's tough
Remember how Jesus died for you
    He also had it rough.
But while He lived He taught
    Us how to survive from day to day
He taught us first to love everyone
    To work and watch and pray
So hang in there and keep on pushing
    And the victory you'll win
For Jesus Christ the Son of God
    Will always be your friend.

Review Questions

1. Name the Adults that you can trust. Ask Mom or Dad to help you make your list.

2. Who are some strangers you can trust? (Pgs. 6-8)

   Can you think of any other strangers you can trust?

3. Who are your best friends?

4. Who do you trust with your secrets and why?

5. What are two main rules about trust to remember? (Pg. 4)

6. Who should you talk to when you're not sure what you should do? (Pg. 4)

7. There are times when your family and friends can't be there for you. Who loves you very much and is always there for you? (Pg. 16)

Scriptures Referring to Trust

Scriptures are quoted first from the **King James** version, then the **Living Bible.**

Though He slay me, yet will I trust in Him:
But I will maintain mine own ways before Him.

God may kill me for saying this—in fact, I expect Him to.
Nevertheless I am going to argue my case with Him.

(Job 13:15)

Blessed is that man that maketh the Lord his
trust, and respecteth not the proud, nor such
as turn aside to lies.

Many Blessings are given to those who trust
the Lord, and have no confidence in those
who are proud, or who trust in idols.

(Ps. 40:4)

It is better to trust in the Lord than to put
confidence in Man.

It is better to trust in the Lord than to put
confidence in Man.

(Ps. 118:8)

But mine eyes are unto Thee, O God the Lord:
In Thee is my trust: Heave not my soul
destitute.

I look to you for help, O Lord God. You are
my refuge. Don't let them slay me.

(Ps. 141:8)

Who is among you that feareth the Lord, that
obeyeth the voice of his servant, that
walketh in darkness and hath no light? Let
him trust in the name of the Lord, and stay
upon his God.

Who among you fears the Lord and obeys His
servant? If such men walk in darkness, without
one ray of light, let them trust the Lord.
Let them rely upon their God.

(Isa. 50:10)

Take ye heed every one of his neighbors, and
trust ye not in any brother: for every
brother will utterly supplant, and every
neighbor will walk with slanders.

Beware of your neighbor! Beware of your
brother! All take advantage of one another
and spread their slanderous lies.

(Jer. 9:4)

Trust ye not in a friend, put ye not
confidence in a guide: Keep the doors
of thy mouth from her that lieth in
thy bosom.

Don't trust anyone, not your best friend.

(Mic. 7:5)

The Lord is good, a strong hold in the day
of trouble; and He knoweth them that trust
in Him.

The Lord is Good. When trouble comes, He is
the place to go! And He knows everyone who
trusts in Him.

(Nah. 1:7)

And the disciples were astonished at his words.
But Jesus answereth again, and saith
unto them, "Children, How hard is it for them
that trust in riches to enter into
the Kingdom of God."

This amazed them. So Jesus said it again:
"Dear children, how hard it is for those who
trust in riches to enter the Kingdom of God."

(Mark 10:24)

And He spake this parable unto certain which
trusted in themselves that they were
righteous, and despised others.

Then he told this story to some who boasted
of their virtue and scorned everyone else.

(Luke 18.9)

For therefore we both labor and suffer
reproach because we trust in the Living God,
Who is the Saviour of all Men, specially of
Those that believe.

We work hard and suffer much in order that
People will believe it, for our hope is in
the Living God who died for all, and
Particularly for those who have accepted
His salvation.

(I Tim. 4:10)

Biblical References

Scriptures are quoted first from the **King James** version, then the **Living Bible**.

And, ye Fathers, provoke not your children to
wrath; but bring them up in the nurture and admonition
of the Lord.

And now a word to you parents. Don't keep
on scolding and nagging your children, making
them angry and resentful. Rather, bring
them up with the loving discipline the Lord
himself approves, with suggestions and
Godly advice.

(Eph. 6:4)[1]

Children, obey your parents in the Lord:
For this is right.

Children, obey your parents; this is the right thing
to do because God has placed them in authority over you.

(Eph 6:1)[2]

And Jesus, when He was baptized, went up
straightway out of the water: and, lo, the
heavens were opened unto Him, and He saw
the spirit of God descending like a dove, and
lighting upon Him: And lo a voice from
heaven saying, **"This is my beloved Son,
in whom I am well pleased."**

After His baptism, as soon as Jesus came up
out of the water, the heavens were opened to
Him and he saw the spirit of God coming down
in the form of a dove. And a voice from
heaven said, **"This is my beloved Son, and I
am wonderfully pleased with Him."**

(Matt. 3:16-17)[3]

And I say unto you, Ask, and it shall be given you; seek,
and ye shall find; knock, and it shall be opened unto you.

For every one that asketh receiveth; and he that seeketh
findeth; and to him that knocketh it shall be opened.

If a son shall ask bread of any of you that is a father,
will he give him a stone? Or is he ask a fish, will he for
a fish will he give him a serpent?

Or if he shall ask an egg, will he offer him a scorpion?

If ye then, being evil, know how to give good gifts unto your
children: how much more shall your heavenly Father give the
Holy Spirit to them that ask Him?

And so it is with prayer—keep on asking and you will keep
on getting; keep on looking and you will keep on finding;
knock and the door will be opened.

Everyone who asks, receives; all who seek, find; and the door is opened to everyone who knocks.

You men who are fathers—if your boy asks for bread, do you give him a stone? If he asks for fish, do you give him a snake?

If he asks for an egg, do you give him a scorpion? Of course not!

And if even sinful persons like yourselves give children what they need, don't you realize that your heavenly Father will do at least as much, and give the Holy Spirit to those who ask Him?"

(Luke 11:9-13)[4]